Fishing in the Devonian

Fishing in the Devonian

Carol Jenkins

PUNCHER & WATTMANN

© Carol Jenkins 2008

This book is copyright. Apart from any fair dealing for the purposes of study and research, criticism, review or as otherwise permitted under the Copyright Act, no part may be reproduced by any process without written permission. Inquiries should be made to the publisher.

First published in 2008

Published by Puncher and Wattmann
PO Box 441
Glebe NSW 2037

http://www.puncherandwattmann.com
puncherandwattmann@bigpond.com

National Library of Australia
Cataloguing-in-Publication entry:

Jenkins, Carol
1958 -
Fishing in the Devonian
ISBN   9781921450099
I. Title.
A821.3

Cover design by Matthew Holt

Printed by McPhersons Printing Group

This project has been assisted by the Australian Government through the Australia Council, its arts funding and advisory body.

Contents

Fishing in the Devonian	9
Cloud Me	10
Disorders of Belief	11
PET Facts	12
Flat-Pack	13
Peace comes dropping slow	14
Re-moved States	15
When Years Take the Stars Away	16
The Yard	17
Two times tables	19
Chaired	21
Narrative Elements	22
Mad Mary shucking fast dozens,	24
A Life in Fridges	25
Let the loneliness roll in	32
For the Road	33
Rogation Night	34
After living together for a year	35
Slow Mirror	36
Clays Bookshop – Kings Cross	37
Trade-ins: Small Arms	38
Test Walk	39
How Much	40
Dispossessing	41
Kulin Seasons	43
Toy People	46
Continuing presence of sky	48

Pollen	49
A Short Treatise on Dew/ Seventeen Difficult Questions to Ask	51
Jigsaw	53
Orange Esters on a Tree Dark Morning	54
Artefact from a dream of happiness	55
The Weave (1786)	56
The Blessings of Saint Vincent	57
Short Boots	58
Getting ready for the cold	59
Over Winter	60
Silk Pyjamas	61
Silkweeds	62
Behind the Scenes at Willow City	63
Hot Chocolate	66
Lifebuoy	68
Fifteen Tangents	69
Carver's Graveyard Tour	70
Architrave	71
White Poem No 4: Ode to the Potato	72
three puzzle pieces	73
Night Croquet	75
On a backwater eBay in Seyfert's Galaxy	76
Excerpts from the Dictionary of Vago Masli	79
Last night, lying there	81

To my sister and brothers

Acknowledgments

Grateful acknowledgment is made to the editors of the following journals, anthologies and programs in which some of these poems were first published: *Antipodes, Cordite, Blue Dog, Famous Reporter, foam:e, Heat, Ilumina, Island, Meanjin, Nth Position, Overland, Poetica, Quadrant, Snorkel, Southerly, The Merri Creek, Tirra Lirra* and *Writers Radio.*

My thanks also to my publisher David Musgrave, Michael Sharkey, Matthew Holt, Greg McLaren, Alphabeticals, The Sunday Poetry Group, Judith Beveridge and Stephen Nettleton.

Fishing in the Devonian

Try Ellesmere Island when it's green and still attached
to Greenland. One fish, *Tiktaalik roseae,* is having second
thoughts about the water, it's perfectly clean
but there is the attractive ooze of mudflats
with morsels of scorpions and millipedes,
though you can't say millipedes in the Devonian
as there are no fingers to count on or Greek
prefixes for one thousand. The fish are inclined
to muddiness, mud not being much of a flavour
even for Devonians. How they throng
up and over the shore on their lobed fins, so maybe
you don't have to throw a line in, in the classic sense
because that *Tiktaalik* is trying its best to get out,
get the morning papers and have a neck to look around.
Devonian fish come in metres so consider
scrupulously the best kind of hook and bait,
what kind of gloves you need to get that hook out.

Perhaps don't go out in a small boat built
of spongy Devonian wood – not much
by way of secondary thickening
though a stout source of carbon. There is a lot
to think about in fishing in the Devonian. So,
pack thoughtfully.

Cloud Me

Written on the 30th anniversary of *The Selfish Gene*

With the clouding factor of being here,
in this brilliant light, and not being with you,
the blue bouncing like love gone crazy around the room,

I stand on the scales, at sea level,
with all the gravity I can muster, divide by ten
and multiply by seven to approximate my liquidity,

that was once, and will be, pure cloud.
I read as thirty-eight litres of cloud potential,
thirty-eight litres of ebullient cumulus rising,

lapping through the water cycle I will be nimbus,
stratus, cirrus, altos, storm and ice.
We'll mix, rise, condense together, travel and rain apart,

separate from the DNA that codes for bones and muscles
to tilt a head that might revert to thinking about clouds,
and needs a body to bear it.

While those little squirls of code, the selfish species subsets,
swim to extinction, my enduring water,
returning cloud shaped, will outlast all organic parts of me.

Disorders of Belief

She wanted to believe in vanilla,
its falling edge dream state,
wanted to believe in Mr Whippy happiness
melting white rivulets down her fingers.

She wanted to believe in natural science, aeration
and emulsification without chemical flocculants,
built up with a froth of air, like the way
she felt his conduit to her limbic.

She wanted to believe in beneficent medicine,
in the afternoon light with trees lit like props
for novellas and clouds which she could pile
into a cone to take as extravagant placebos.

She wanted to believe in bone, muscle, blood,
skin and pheromones but ran into the anaesthetic
of romance, the predisposition to delusional
sexually receptive states, where ova fell like manna
into libido and swindled the shoes from her feet,
when they should have echoed on a distant floor.

She had problems with belief:
with him, with God and the way she thought
love might be medicine but was an awkward sickness.
Her disorder is to trust the placebo
of what she thinks he thinks
over believing what he says,
because God she can do without.

PET[1] Facts

In an experiment with radioactive glucose,
Area 25, PET scanning and 'Terms of Endearment'
neurologists have located the Sadness Centre

in the brain, where tiny families sit
down for afternoon tea when the baby
dies at the hospital

and a woman stands looking out
the window saying it's over, it's over
under her breath.

It has an empty bookshelf, the first Christmas card
you ever made for Dear Mummy
and a handkerchief.

They have found a little door
to the Sadness Centre and with the help
of an electrode they can put a closed sign

on the door to tell the thoughts
that want to hang around and be miserable
that no-one's home and *don't come back either.*

---

[1] PET – Positron Emission Tomatography

Flat-Pack

Keats starts off his new life folding instructions for Ikea
flat-pack furniture, studies physics at night school,
buys a child ticket to take his bicycle
on a romantic train trip, begins to understand
negative capability in the railway overpass,
and folds things with poetry.

Out in Padstow, a 43 year old female cabalist,
who has squeezed a flat pack dark cherry veneer
computer desk into her apartment, unfolds
the assembly instructions, and finds a dark universe
is continuing to accelerate from the single sheet
of photon paper, which becomes – sequentially –
a bicycle, a child, a ticket and instructions
on how to live as, or on, or by, a cherry wood
desk, a farm, a tea chest and any planet
that has atmosphere.

Peace comes dropping slow

In a trance he mops the one he remembers
onto the hospice floors at Coole, adding a line,
and erasing it with quick light strokes.
Late nights, he refines his calligraphy
of trailing edges, skims the Wild Swans
across the lake of linoleum,
and nudges small eddies of broken water
around the chair legs in the Emergency Waiting Room.

A nurse finds she is counting heart beats
to his measure, and in the lub dub of diastole,
systole, there seems to be, beneath the steady beat,
a movement like the heart's wild
swerve, that might resolve into
a tearing satisfaction before it stops.

Re-moved States

'Imagine if all that light that fell on you, bouncing
off as it does, with the impression of you
running forward into films and eyes
and digital cameras, but, as it can't all be caught,
some part of you keeps racing off
past those that are watching. Maybe
it keeps going out into the air and into space
like radio waves, only much quieter.
Somewhere, light-years away
there might be a silver nitrate planet
and all over the surface there are these
people's images, and they look real
but a little exhausted by the journey and they don't
realise they are images – projected
shadows – and think they are talking
and kissing, making love and reading,
but they're only particles: well that's what
the gods think, what they laugh about
when they watch us.'
Maki announces this to me one morning,
and then he laughs. 'Oh,' I say, 'Maki
I know you're imaginary,'
but then he does this thing with his eyebrows
– so human – and I wonder about him too.

When Years Take the Stars Away

If you're reading this in one-hundred-million,
two-thousand and seven AD, that is, after all the stars
have inched away, taking their tails of light with them,
far off to where the universe strikes a light against
what, at the time of writing, has no dimension, the timeless
place that time is coming to, I want to tell you
that here – right now – the sky is prinked
with nebulae in clusters and symposia,
the light is mostly white, so you get the true idea of blackness
and the abundance is such that it presses infinities
into the foreheads of children lying safe in their beds at night,
and those who can get out from the cities
and take the time to sit outside, make up elaborate
stories, concerning these embroideries of starlight, and if
a meteorite rushes, burning, into the Earth's air,
wonderment bubbles up, into this strange satisfaction
which might be happiness. I want you to know, as you sit
reading this on your black and starless planet
that you should not find that blank
blanket of night a reason to believe that stars do not exist,
the galaxies, the Milky Ways and the jewel of Magellan's Clouds,
still shine and burn abundant in distant orbits.

The Yard

Beyond the domestic grass
and Jacaranda, past May Bush,
kero tins of thyme, sage, queen
of herbs, a gate that never closed

the bottle yard's snaky path,
an eighteen inch width, warm
sand that gets between your toes,
mica specked with darker glints,

adheres with stubborn greyness,
comes with you past the stacks,
through heat souring remnant
wine to vinegar and yeast lapsed

bottle dregs, fermentations in a glass world
dizzy with spirit pungents, wine
and whiskey interlopers here in a landscape ruled
by beer and the slung up percussion

of a dozen dozen bottles' clashing symphonic
sway of glass, the syncopated clink
and ring of one hundred and twenty-one nestled
empty browns that sing a glass syntax,
a bright cadence of fast onset,

slurring over frequency, they pitch a little,
lilt not quite united to a slow fading
empty bottle echo.

A block away at school I can sort by ear
what they're loading, mostly or strictly
brown for brewery trucks.
Greens and special shapes, rare blues

antique cobalts, iridescent greens with marble
stoppered throats opalised by entombment,
disinterred in strange digs are kept

for admiration, like the kiddies' prize of plastic Scotties
— black and white. I learn to count
in halfpenny browns — they pay
in a world mapped out in empties.

Two times tables

A thunderstorm circles the house, blue-greenish —
the schoolyard paddock across the road
is an amphitheatre lit by branding light,
and the sky's tearing itself to bits.
In the open doorway
— where she has said we would be electrocuted,
she sits, legs out straight, head turned skyward,
fat rain drops steam summer heat
from the concrete porch, and I watch her, watching
and I can't bear it and say come away from the door,
the lightning could get you,
'I don't care, it can,' she says.
She might be thirty or thirty one, and I'm
pleading with her but she doesn't move, she is getting
wet and any moment could be hit by lightning.

Six years later she shuts herself into the walk-in wardrobe
with a large knife, muttering that she's not
going to cut her wrists,
but on account of how sharp
the knife is and the way her voice tapers off
to this frantic pitch, I know at twelve,
holding my two months
baby sister, that it would be a good idea to
get her, or the knife,
out of the wardrobe.
My elder brother and I coax and beg,
plead, argue and cajole, and she cries
and goes on and on,
the baby cries, and we talk about stuff
and say she can stay in there
but can she please give us the knife.

Chaired

I loved the wooden chair - the slats at the back
with a gap just big enough for me
 to squeeze my head into.
I was five years old, talking to my parents
— it was perfectly normal and weird —
that I was caught — kneeling on the kitchen floor
behind the chair, with my head sticking
through the slats just above the grainy polish of the seat

After I little while I asked, politely,
for some help to get out. My father
torn between lunch and laughing, offered
to saw the chair in half. My mother
merely laughed, as if I was TV,
and sat down at the table.

After a while I scraped my ears off
(practically) and got out, teary,
auricles red and throbbing. Improbably,
I was glad the chair was still all one piece.

Narrative Elements

I spend a whole poem writing *I want to quit
the narrative habit.* It doesn't work.

As soon as I could read I was interested in labels,
and frequently stood on a chair to consider De Witts'
Kidney Pills but never figured it out. The pills were grey
and oblate.

Ashton's Circus would set up at Ettalong Oval each year
for a few weeks, if you were lucky you'd see an elephant
go past on a truck.

A teacher called Mr Quinley slapped my legs for walking
into him in the corridor. I was eight and prone to day dream.

The green grocers didn't have zucchinis
and I was puzzled about the word eggplant.

At primary school they said we lived in a dormitory suburb.
There was no suggestion of irony, so it was true.

My cousin wanted me to stand in the driveway with her
and throw blue metal at my neighbour's car. Her father
was committing adultery with the neighbour. We were ten. I said no.

In Fifth Class I got an autograph book for my birthday,
and if my friends asked what they should write in it I would tell
them. 'That's a nice one,' my Aunt said, pointing,
it was no use explaining.

In Sixth class I took an overdose of valium, two milligram
tablets but I can't remember how many. Maybe six.
I weighed about five stone and slept till the next day.

I made packet self-saucing puddings for dessert
to follow the Sunday roast. I knew how to make
gravy, white onion sauce and dumplings.

A boy in my first year high school class sent
me a postcard from Papua New Guinea,
don't write, he said, *the natives might notice.*

I had plenty of friends, all the time, nice girls too.
Sometimes I'd go home for lunch, so they could
have someone to talk about. They needed narrative.

Mad Mary shucking fast dozens,

muttering. Henry, bigger than a bread and butter
plate, hoisted up for inspection at the lease,
lemons floating in the punt bilge.

Hessian sacks stitched up rough,
like smiles with broken teeth
that never made it past a pub without a drink.

The drawer with a dozen oyster knives
in every different house.

Matthew in a high chair after lunching
on mulberries, oysters and salami,
the headache in his belly.

The sweet, salt freshness,
the living days on land,

and the bitter cream, the shell
& tin electrolyte of the bad ones.

A Life in Fridges

I
For some reason, maybe the kero fume, the first fridge
is nicotine yellow. Naturally it hisses.
If I go close my nose stops working
and there is a taste of blueness
in the back of my throat.
The space for food seems to be about a small
cupboard's worth.
It takes my father and two other men
to get it out of the kitchen.

II
We get the Pope. It is white and electric
and has a freezer space. I spend some time
opening the door to feel the engagement
and disengagement of the catch.
The term *shut the door* comes into
common parlance. A long series of explosions,
brown foamy detonations of beer
bottles, commence. Ice-cream bricks and sharded glass
inhabit a space with the white smell of aluminium
ice-cube trays.

III
In a year of plenty the two-door arrives, notable
for its butter conditioner, a warm enclave
in the clean-lit brightness. There are egg holders,
a meat tray. There is more room in the freezer
which is given over to beer mugs.
One day I am helping clean the fridge
and break the hinged door of the butter conditioner.
For years the broken hinges mock
my clumsiness.

IV
When I leave home there are two weeks with no fridge
and then someone's old beer fridge
is dragged dripping, like adulthood,
into the kitchen of McEvoy Ave. At first it is empty
and coughs mechanically, a late
night shudder, as if dreaming it forgot how
to breathe and then the motor kicks back in
and gets on with it.

V
In a furnished Norwood flat, the fridge door
holds one jar of apricot jam,
cyanic from too much kernel. Abandoned,
it leavens, into a luminous carotene,
and precociously over-ripens into alcohol – I made that.

VI

22A Stafford Street, three rooms one after
the other, a semi without the luxury
of a hallway or a fridge. Emeric from 22
comes to drone Canook at me. While I
wrestle my first sourdough his heart infarcts.
I call the ambulance to avoid resuscitating his blue lips.
Both he and the bread turn out OK.
While he is in hospital I disinter his fridge,
and install it in my kitchen, removing
from its empty chest a heart-attack
grey chop. The smell of sauerkraut persists.

VII

Over time I learn how coldness will squeeze
water from the air, watch the inversion of space to ice,
observe the insulating inefficiency of hard frost.
I become a student of defrosting, work at the ice's weak points
with bone-handled dinner knives and solid plate irons,
still plugged in, sear, hissing through the ice,
frayed cotton cords sodden. I attack with pots of boiling water,
graduate to hair dryers and blunt instruments,
mop up with too-quickly stiffening sponges
and wet wrung tea-towels, ice-slurry bunds of old bath towels
and the satisfaction of the freezer ice-roof caving in,
the kitchen sink a pewter white geography of melt.

VIII

An upstairs flat, above a shop on King William Street
with me independent of the polloi.
One of the two kind men friends herniated
while bearing this one's dead weight
up a Marlene Dietrich case of wooden stairs.

IX

A white casket of dubious biologic interior,
the outside a billboard, for word of the day
and noms-de-plume e.g.: rodomontade,
and Hugo-escargot-o, the fish that waltzed;
on a kitchen floor underpinned by termites.

X

In Darlinghurst it seems so adult
to buy a fridge from the last white goods
shop on Oxford Street. One day I find,
on its crown plateau of dust and bills,
in an old fruit bowl, a banana
as black and limp as stout.
Weeks later I move out.

XI

The resident fridge in Newtown creaks open
on a boy's own chop style of cooking,
but there is something in the air, I move in
and the fridge shortly transmogrifies into a glorious
and complex food confusion of greens
and cheeses, quail, pancetta, blue-swimmer crabs,
dark caramelled lemon chutney, fat ovals
of whisky chocolate cakes, sauv blancs and ice smashed
up for Cointreau, and on high feast days
the bathroom's ice-bagged into a cold store.

XII

When I get to his flat, I am drawn to the bar-size fridge
and in slow-slow motion open it
despite knowing he is watching me intrude.
I bend over Alice-like, my eyes Polaroids,
and even now I can still see that one ice-berg lettuce
and the packet of chilled Latina ravioli.

XIII

Life is upside down, so is the fridge.

A new baby and the freezer fills with yellow bottles

their mosaic icy fractals radiating paler lines. After

the first positive test run, I stock pile these every day

(flow rate can't be episodic) and they stay in the freezer –

bar the first test none of that expressed milk is ever used.

Above the freezer line, the fridge shelves prove unstable,

I become adroit at catching a sliding mass of jars and Décor

plastic boxes, arms loaded, chest and knees doing what they can

to cope with these surprises.

XIV

The magnets come, the first twenty six

are the bloody alphabet which I pick up

about a thousand times a week,

then a wooden cow, novelty fruit,

the ad rectangles for plumbers and pest

exterminators, all exert degrees of attraction

through the drawings, photos, shopping lists,

in a quadratic that pitches gravity, surface area

and depth of field against magnetics.

XV

In a cascade of misadventures and consumer-itis a megalitre
ice-making HCFC depot plumbs into the house – it grinds
its teeth, gear locks, and cognates out ice cubes; if pressed it will
gristle ice in fin-de-siecle-ish crush-upon-demand.
Inside it's an overpopulated wasteland, a bank of food,
it's everything: three kinds of yoghurt, five chutneys,
six varieties of soft cheeses, a Tardis trail through dark matter,
time and meals. And then again it's Boyle's fridge, as the items
that need refrigerating gaseously expand to fill it.
It's magnetic, pluralistic, and that's before the doors
swing open. Outside is a public documentation of family life;
of the inside, I say to visitors, don't open that fridge,
it's like my unconscious, there are good things in there
and some things you will not want to know.
To illustrate this, and that the term vegetable crisper
is an oxymoron, I gently lever up a liquid zucchini,
fizzing slightly yellow, photograph it and post this on the door.

Let the loneliness roll in

Steppenwolf seeps, like fog, from the borrowed ute's
cassette player as I watch Mark drive. We are driving
from Woy Woy to Armidale – a weekend away.
He is twenty-five, I'm seventeen, and we are lovers.

The road unzips beneath us. He concentrates
with persuasive intensity. I stare out the window
at the straggly eucalypts. Steppenwolf's Foggy Mental

Breakdown slides into the bridge. 'No,' my father
had said. I said, 'I'm going.' When I look back
at Mark, it all inverts, he peels away from everything
in my control and takes the world with him.

For the Road

First as a dare and then for the warm languor
of the tar, at midnight walking to my house,
we lay down our bodies on the middle
of Moana Road and kissed, those long dreamy
kisses of abandonment, to each other, to the road,
to the dark pines looking on, to the locked light
of houses with blinds drawn tight on quarter acre
blocks, the stars' bright and dizzy mass
arcing over us, and we'd get to our feet, like angels
coming to in a strange world, to walk
down the road, arms and hands tangling,
laughing, like we'd swallowed a universe
and it was exploding out of our fingertips.

Rogation Night

After weeks dedicated to sheening skin with sweat,
evenings squandered to drown the mouth,
hours mesmerized by the marginalia of cells
separating lip from skin, long minutes lost exploring
accretions bonded to the fine long hairs in his armpit,
come the epochs that map crab ecologies of pubis,
the bones of the face, the heat inside the throat.

We navigate time by the dense smell of swamped
sheets, lick salt clocks from lids and eyelashes,
read the fine print of finger on finger.
We are tongue-tied, each flex and contraction
of muscle a reflex, and silk blood floods the gorge,
so it is impossible to walk, or think
without feeling every hours' residue. I am lying,
staring at a throb of stars, till the pale moon
of a forties dressing table bounces the street light
round the fibro walls.

I'm hungry and whisper to him, he says Yes,
but that we should fuck without any part of us touching,
except clit, cunt and cock.

He balances over me, pulling away if I move in,
giving measure when I don't,
I sit up front wards, balancing, working into him
a sliding pivot of slow quickening, where ascension
and desire blaze as saints, the skin pleads
and as crooked as street light travelling backwards,
time splinters to sharp fastness and pierces
deep into the dark interior of the room.

After living together for a year

I teach him to knit. He knits,
tight, exact, the yarn's
stretch and give are gone,
this is wool as metal work.
No stitch is given slack.
I take up the small oblong,
feel in it the tensile density
of his abdomen —
it's venous, rushing up my arm,
as the blue magnet of his eyes
runs the line between us
as taut as the next noose
off the needle.

Slow Mirror

In the afternoon, while the shower
runs a temperature, I undress and
watch my body, slow watch

my mirrored hand fit the planes
and muscles, the flat curves
of abdomen and hold the moment

of my breast, like watching clouds
or eating grapes when the teeth
edge through the skin

to the lie of sweetness
on the tongue, in all of these
the slow mirror of your mouth.

Clays Bookshop — Kings Cross

It's 1984 and one hundred dollars is in excess
of generous for a voucher. It seems certain,
even before I place it quietly on the counter,
that Miss Chapman, who has deduced the complexity
of what I like and want and should read, will find out.

She casts an eye from it to Judith Menzies, who steps over,
and they both look at the voucher. A blush is moving
from my throat to my face — 'Oh,' Miss Chapman says,
and I can hear her eyebrows rising but on her face
they are obedient to her person, 'we wondered,' and here
Judith M. concurs — 'we wondered who that Young Man
belonged to' — her hand describes a vivid arc, 'oh he bounced
and sprang around the shop — in a way we talked about for days,
so exuberant and charming,' and both she and her hand stop short,
and we get down to business, 'but we did not think it could be you
— we thought… that young man who's always with you…'

For a moment I study the Reference Section, and then I say,
'Oh, I work with James, and I live with Mark,'
and like mirrors with a time delay, one eyebrow
of Judith Menzies' reflects that of Miss Chapman,
who stretches out the words, 'Well, you are lucky,'
smiles at me, and at that moment, maybe I am.

Trade-ins: Small Arms

And then there is the soft innocence of small arms,
the round oval of the wrist/stock, the clarity of skin/metal,
the single crease inside the elbow/trigger that tells it.

'What happens to the rest of the body
when they've sold the arms?' – at eight, he asks,
after listening to us talk.

In Colombia the militia might slit the skin
of his forehead or pectoral to pack in brown-brown
– raw amphetamine – and top up this charge
with booze and ganja, so fear cannot be found
in any of the atoms left in his eight-year old head.
He'd be given orders, a machete, an M16 –
a light child-sized innocent sort of small arm,
– ex-US Excess Defense. He would find
the answer is, once the arm is severed at the shoulder
or wrist, – short or long-sleeve as they say –
a man, a woman or a child, will live or bleed to death.

Test Walk

In Atlanta a man takes a prosthetic leg
for a test walk and does not come back.

When I am six I find my Great Uncle Sid's
tin leg alone in the hall. He is asleep in the next room.

In Afghanistan a girl touches the wing of a green
parrot and her hand flies off.

Sid's leg is the fleshy pink of tinned salmon.

Centres in Baghdad, Basra and Najef supported by the
International Committee of the Red Cross fit 11,956 prostheses.

Watching boys playing handball, a mother in Mosman remarks
that library fines for overdue books cost an arm and a leg.

How Much

So beautiful that I know she does not fit in.
The pale skin, the dark red willow of her hair,
she is the Doctor's wife and quite hopeless.
I am sent there overnight, a child,
by my mother, and don't fit in with any
of her four. One largish girl sits on my chest.
The air inside me leaves and for a moment
as it stays away, I might be dying slowly,
at least from mortification.

The smallest, who at two survived sleeping in the bath,
– nose and mouth just above the tide of it,
eats runny custard – as do the other three –
with two fingers, spooning slurps of yellow.
I watch their mother to see where the edge
of her nervous insouciance recedes.

Years later, when she throws herself
– perfect body, less one breast –
off the cliff, onto the rocks,
I go on to wonder how much
self one needs.

Dispossessing

the years of collection, walls
nacreous from hoardings, a paper
codex, squirrelings, till each room,

a labyrinth of the past, teeters
ceiling to floor with extracted
life, objectified, amassed, meant,

grows out to clog the doors
packs down the hallway,
extrudes into the garage, engulfs
a car, morphs towards the street

this refuge for roadside discards knows
all the damp sufferings of domestic
disintegration, the decay
of possibilities for:

baskets, doll houses, tins, cupboards,
chairs, lowboys, blinds, plastic toy
lawnmowers, upholstered blanket
boxes, ornaments, a model elephant, wicker
side tables, pots, decades of newspaper

when the grey wisps pump out
from the side of the house, grey blood
rising furious at past containment

everything there comes into itself
the house, the stacks, the compacts
with rancid fat and frayed electrics

all the puttings-up with of the floor
the doors, frame work, roof and
tiles, all conspire, cease to be shelter
and go with the loading
to make too much fuel
for any fire to continue to resist

heat, fervent heat and plenty of it,
billows of pumping smoke,
carbon unbounded

glass exploding, a fire music,
as windows hammer out
a percussive map, bits of ash, cinders, specks,
newspaper coins floating off

a fire engine pissing itself
like a red cow on bitumen

dozens of red blue lights rotate
in scenic hypnosis, everything
a filter of smoke, strobes,
sirens, engine burble
takes over as sound

young men in suits ask the voyeurs,
do you live here?

Kulin Seasons

This poem is for the Kulin people, in the cold Yarra Valley, who found these seven seasons of place and for others who have found seven marketing events, with thanks to Museum Victoria's Forest Exhibit.

Buath Garr, the pobblebonk calls,
its voice a falling stone
in the moist twilight that wraps
long grass round your legs.

Shopping malls pre-emptively bleat carols;
you are sent reeling for your plastic &
buy snowmen cards to send to people you
don't talk to.

In kangaroo-apple season
you can watch small bats
harvesting insects from twilight.

Or behold Christmas's bleakly dancing bear,
eat and drink too much, such fun
is seldom seen.

Close on, the Southern Cross is
low and level on the horizon
it's Biderup, the dry season:
the heat in the day hangs on your shoulders
and shade is improbably cooler.

We have the summer sales
when clothes are racked and wheeled out to shop fronts
and breezy banners announce red hot specials
to match the pouting weather.

Iuk comes, fat eels swimming
towards Canopus in the east,
the manna gum is flowering,
perfect weather for new lovers.

Previews of winter fashions
stumble drunk and prickly hot
into shop windows:
now is the time
to buy long pants of wool.

Waring, wombat season:
wombats walk as if the inheritors
of the earth, days
are short to suit wombat legs.

We are flooded with foiled
compounded chocolate, cheap
yellow chicks and motifs of feral cuteness
as the expressways boil with Easter drivers.

If they only knew that orchid season is coming,
much would be gained
by a careful study of the forest floor
while walking quietly with friends.

The winter sales are declared,
all the clothes are now at the right temperature —
pity they don't have your size.

We might slip into tadpole season
where days and nights are balanced,
the stars are judicious, things go right.

Or restock the warrior father's larder
with power tools and update
to wider viewing screens.

But somewhere the grass is flowering again;
warm rain is falling and at dusk
Orion stands sentry to the east.

Toy People

Scientists report they have
found remains of toy people
on Flores Island
and the journalists add
they were pea brains
that hunted miniature elephants
which scientist Peter Brown
said would make nice pets.

It was variably reported
that they were too stupid
to talk, or could talk
which was amazing because
they were so stupid.

Either they were just smart
enough to build a boat
after they talked about it
or light enough to swim
a long way, and mercifully
the lack of language prevented
them from complaining
about the weather, weariness and sharks.

They were all wiped out
by a volcano 15,000 years ago
but it might be that the last died
only 500 years ago.

Island stories say
in old times food was left out
for the Little People
and they ate everything
including the gourds.

But maybe they took
the gourds and after some discussion
used them to build a better boat
to travel a place where the Big People
weren't so patronizing,
or could at least
get the story straight.

Continuing presence of sky

Yesterday four men
came and installed more
sky in the gully. It was messy
and noisy, and they left
a great spread of chainsaw
dust and two plank benches.
Who would have known
the sky came wrapped in wood?

Pollen

Down-scale gene lifeboat, wind shifted silt,
nose teaser, sneeze bearer, deciduous dust,
anther emblem, furtive clinger, protein panicle,
bee money, corbicula cruiser,
twitching yellow, gold-white and red dust

    I love the mode of you

miniature lolly bag beauty, purveyor of fragrance,
haploid peddler of running tears, fertiliser,
petal stain, persistent infiltrator,
geologic indicia, independent gamete
that shivers flower quim to the base

    I love the sex of you

thecal sleeper, totemic plant shadow,
Laib carpet, ubiquitous botanic ambassador
in topaz, yellow, persimmon and deep
dust of pinkness, diminutive deep grooved
grain with wrinkled rock melon coat,

    I love the art of you

baby cheezel, spiky mini-pod with
pores, nucleoli, cellulose thickening under
your intine clothed in a Jacobean exine coat,
palynologic mapper of fossil landscape,
night rider of the western lyric

    I love your logic

metronome of hay fever, wind strategist,
resister of decomposition, pack rat fossil,
paisley print meniscus pond patterner
lying as taxonomic code
in bog, fen, marsh and microscope

    I love the float,
    the sink, the grit of you.

A Short Treatise on Dew/ Seventeen Difficult Questions to Ask

What were you expecting other than to feel numbness glide
into your soles, as your shoes grew damp, the heaviness of longing
eating into the leather?

You stare and want to make some statement about the oblate drop —
the surface is the trick — it concentrates, candling water
from the air: does this obliterate any requirement for exchange?

Slink beads on bottles and car bonnets — you are as lovely to the tongue
as paradox, those cold kisses that glaze and the cat sitting
hot/damp on the engine — did I ask if you purred?

If all the other people/ drops are removed,
does this make the field better or worse?

Do you remember the first words we spoke, spiked with intent
already condensed to a double statement?

Do you want those days of drenching beauty — where privacy slides
across the surface tension, rink after gliding rink, the effortless grace
of the return cross over, the ice spray, soft as chamois?

Droplets form around these compositional irritations, nuances
of dialect, weep points. What is the purpose in trying not to love
that clear glistening? Dew is tears the air abandons wantonly
on the face of things.

A gently stealing influence — time is implicit in dew — when did this
start, this giddiness and dampness between the blades of your legs?

Dew forms to join air and surface, like lips in the briefest, lightest
of kisses — can you taste night on your lips?

Canopy or tree dew acts like hosannas, settling lightly
and then leaving without touching the ground:
is this a model you aspire to?

Dew is a system of give and take, some days the grass drinks it in
and other days the air takes it back — this is not like an apology.
Have you studied this to learn
how to make those disguised transitions?

We live in this dilute ocean of air and water which is invisible,
like love. Do you ever get this feeling that you are wreathed
by damp bonds?

Dew-sprung grass, dew burning off, adieu, over due, durable:
see what happens when the sun inches in upon a word?

If it all goes un-swimmingly, im-precipitate, dry,
does this withholding seem like you haven't started to live?

Do you feel those secret downpours, collecting from the breath
of words, under tables and telephones,
conversations aggregating in dew ponds?

Will there be a dew-point in our conversation
where language is distilled and without need of words?

If I were to lie in a field overnight, heat radiating from my body,
the fog condensing on the dew-ret linen of my shirt,
would you wake me, and say, it's OK, it was fog, a dream,
there is nothing to say and no answers?

Jigsaw

'So', he says, as I pick up a line
of mountain and sky, 'What will happen
to us when the Sun explodes?'
I say, 'Don't worry we won't be here,'
and find two bits of sky line that fit
together. 'But, he says, will there be people here?'
I say, 'Probably not,' and focus
on where one mountain fits
into the other.

'But it is possible isn't it?'
'Yes, it's possible – it must be possible.'

'Will bits of Sun hit the Earth?'
I say, 'I think the lack of gravity
will have run its course before the Sun
lumps hit the Earth.'
I have tried two dozen ways for one
piece of sky to fit into the mountain.

'Well,' he says, 'it will be bad day,'
watching me, solemn with his skinny
body under a chocolate and cream fleece
blanket, the one I made, with the eyelets
and crosses stitched big.

I leave the puzzle with the sky and mountain
mostly undone, and go over
to wrestle from him the fact of the Sun
exploding and ruining a perfectly good
day on Earth. 'Got you,' he says.

Orange Esters on a Tree Dark Morning

The day starts early, some phantom interloper
firing colour off lows the clouds
to a weasel wrung morning, a little empty
dust scuds under the table, must be spring
season of slammed plates, some great
para-aldehyde, like nature is an artificial
ester, or was the orange blossom
a gag of unrealized patrimony?

If I was better practised at forgetting
you, I wouldn't be so disarmingly apparent
I don't even like the word I, I, I, the whey
of its cheese seepage, the whole remembrance
tulle and Corelli work, a needle needed
to re-sew its spinal misalignments,
for some ripe plucked myth-historic figure
to extemporise, patch over plot lack.

All time is showing off, as if there was a greater
attention to seek, dog-nose like, how hard
to even write the word, sound, image; that asks
me to attend to a thousand phrases, the unapparent bliss,

way out the back – when I look up
into the miasma of trees, in that giddiness
of leaves, there is everything of you.

Artefact from a dream of happiness

All those brave blue mornings that I was,
all those hopelessly soft sunsets
you fell through, the blaze of lastness
with the lake bleeding into twilight's black and white
while the highway sped past all sharp corners,
speed and mesmerism, as something waltzed languid
and wondering through our blood,
burning the idea of ecstasy into a slow reverberatory neural
loop bridging two hemispheres of cells
that was me, the language that we are.

The Weave (1786)

In Richard Walsh's *Book of Ties*
he lists his four dead children.
'Sudden Bright', 'Tabby's Velveret',
'Diamond Handkerchief' stand for Liam,
Rose and Patrick, all too well dosed
with laudanum, and 'Marsh Bird Singing'
this is Eliza, succumbed to Whooping Cough.
These ties he figured, in concentration to keep
his eye off them, propped up behind him, washed, waxen,
waiting for their graves, and he set to, treadle dancing,
weaving by the hour, yards and yards of fancy stuff,
weft surfaced, satin the reverse.

The Blessings of Saint Vincent

Saint Vincent, patron saint of student
clothing, bequeathed to me from the depths

and twists of his sorting tables, a perfect
Victorian camisole, every stitch scaled

in sixteenths of an inch, pin-tucked
lawn and pale silk ribbon that threaded

the three deep inches of lace to play,
across the breasts and shoulder,

a game of hanging on and falling
off and in this antique practice

he gave to me, as skirt and shirt
fell upon floor, something of the feeling

of being both myself and the involuntary
groan of the young man, watching,

waist naked, standing by the bed.

Short Boots

Twenty five dollar boots from Cooks –
on Oxford Street, cow hide,
Cowgirl-style, embossed, with a Cuban
heel, you meant business
and when, at eighteen, I walked
home in the hot compression
of summer after work, the local
mongrels once formed a pack,
the first, hair-sprung snarling, rushed
to introduce his throat to the solid
square of your accelerated toe,
coughed out a little dog blood
while all mine kept pumping,
safe, beneath my skin, dear boots I've
never loved any shoe better
than I loved you then.

Getting ready for the cold

To line my scarf, I hunt out silk satin, that cream
borrower of shades and light, cut to size,
pieces seamed with stitches that slip past like time.
I early learnt to pin, no point tacking
but it's the tension of knit to weave, thread to needle,
the slipping-under-edge, the torsion of what can
stretch to what will not that is the trick.
The knit is prickly but, Oh, the warmth and subtle colour,
the merit in them, and how fine the satin
lights up its borrowed roughness, like my fine face
and skin against the afternoon stubble of your cheek.

Over Winter

I once wore
fine kid gloves and still see
the way the leather holds
the emptiness the hand
has left, hear the glove's
sigh, its endurance as it slowly
exhales the memory of the hand
it held.

Silk Pyjamas

This morning. In oyster grey
silk pyjamas – that once were outerwear.
My lilac cat, my Burmese murderer of birds,
runs his head, an abutment of cloud
soft lilac luxury,
against the silk, against my leg
as I stand, taking in the gully
with its rain, all white grey water
folded in the sky and, unbidden,
images of you descend like winter rain.

Silkweeds

It seems simple and I trust the weight of silk —
the strands' flat lustre that fattens into slub
then regularises as yarn,
laid under, over, in plain weave,
the colour's flax, honey, straw, *raw silk* they say,
— the two words work together
so silk takes all the rawness out of raw.

The fabric glows as if inside the threads
silk worms are reading poetry by lamp light,
couchant in their cocoons. In the dream,
I am wearing a skirt I never had,
explaining that, *No I didn't make it, I can't sew*,
and to demonstrate reveal how the clever seamstress
over-locked the raw edge of flat cut pleats,
and in this dream I believe this manifesto
so absolutely, its moth wings beat
exultant against the inside of my ribs.

But the next morning, and maybe for ever after,
I compare these two contrary weeds:
the dream where silk is skirt and I aver — *I know* —
I am unable to sew;
and the raw silk trousers, worn and made by me,
revived by this dream's sartoriality,
these are true ghosts, two decades old.

Behind the Scenes at Willow City

I In the Kaolin Mine

Chang has spent days, white as death,
cutting stone from Ku-Kou Mountain.
In the torrent he has crushed
the white blocks, washing away
the black veins branching
like deer's-horn seaweed,
before sifting the pai-tun,
now pure white, into bricks of clay
to ferry to the factory.

At night he ties up his boat
and sleeps on the riverbank.

He dreams that he sails under
a willow bridge,
and there is Koong-see
in her cobalt loveliness,
but their feet, the oars, the boat,
won't move, the willow's fall's arrested.
Koong-see's sleeves fold into wings,
Chang finds he cannot speak but sings:
the air puffs out around them.
In this dream he falls asleep
and dreams he is in this same scene,
this same blue, this water stopped,
with Kong-see watching from a painted bridge.

He is leaning out from the little boat,
and cannot bear to look directly
up at her face, her hands, her sleeves
but is entranced with her reflection,
dissolving and re-forming in the river.

II Behind the scenes at Willow City

Koong-see is washing off the cobalt-blue make-up,
packing away the blue clouds,
she is a little stiff from spending so much time
waiting, always waiting
outside the half-moon teahouse, always waiting
for the boat to glide past,
the first willow leaf to flutter down in the light
puffs of ink blue breeze, which must, must come.

After a while she calls across
to the blue porter,
can't you hurry him up?

But the porter stares unblinking,
as still as the doves overhead.

III Morning on the River

Chang wakes damp with dew,
wonders if the dream he dreamt
inside his dream might be
a real dream or the first dream
folded back upon itself?

These thoughts he packs away,
to think of when he and Koong-see
will meet, as he steps in the river,
white clouds of kaolin swirling
from his shirt.

IV Turner's Pottery

Thomas pauses, his fingers tattooed
by copper swarf's sharp tendrils
and ground ink. Under the sway
of willow, he thinks of Ta-jin's jewels
and a Kaoling beauty waiting, silk
hair cascading down, and down
the long whiteness of her back.
He sets his breath and blows
the golden red willow leaves
from the plate, observes their fine
glint in the weak light
of afternoon at Caughly,
and shapes the willow fall
for her.

Hot Chocolate

This is a place with velour upholstered chairs
warm soft chairs that match the placemats
and could be said to match the chintz curtains
if you were colour blind.
It is too cold and late.
An older lady is saying, for a laugh, she
would like to go for a walk by the lake.
Outside, people are wearing coats
and women are holding their husbands' arms.

They give me piped whipped cream
as an adjunct to a big hazelnut danish
and I decide I will not eat the cream.
The next thing I know I dip
a swathe of danish into the cream and eat it.

The girl at the counter asks,
'Do you want your hot chocolate
really, really hot or just really hot?'
'Just normal', replies the girl who wants
hot chocolate.
I imagine a superheated hot chocolate
that creates it own heat vortex,
burning up all the oxygen
in the room and the velour chairs and
the three teenage boys in army fatigues
who have eaten a large bun,
and then burning through the shop
and the mountain underneath it
to make the lake boil.

But maybe that is too much
and it would be more reasonable
for the lake to get to bath temperature
and stay that way,
with the steam curling off it in wisps
in the morning and at night
people would come to watch
the steam rising up to the black sky
and stars shining down.
That would be reasonable.

Lifebuoy

(for emergency use only)

Unless for purpose of lifesaving interference
The sky's grey milk, the wharf is empty
with any lifesaving gear is punishable by a
the baths pitch up an alchemy of cold
penalty of $110 members of the public are
that prohibits swimming in this lilt of water darkening green.
asked to assist in preserving this lifebuoy
June weather crimps my fingers, the air's cold wine
for use when necessary to save life
and walking on I find a disembodied rosella head
By order – the Council of the Municipality of Mosman
and a pink picked clean spine, then, around the corner, wings
to report missing life buoy or vandalism.
still joined, feathers mostly intact, like clothes slipped off.

Fifteen Tangents

I am photographing clouds, they are so hard
to talk to, carrying in an elegiac mass all the words
I didn't say that were perfect for when we weren't
lying together on a paisley cotton quilt, that
your great aunt, who bred silkworms, didn't make.

All those words that sparrows might have pecked at
in the sunshine of a Siennese plaza,
with us counting the stripes on the Duomo,
as their tiny bird feet made our shadows shiver.

When the sky is entirely mocking blue,
like the irony of prefabricated stainless steel,
remember I am not thinking of you,
I'm waiting like Ryogoku Bridge
waited three hundred years for Yoshida
to paint the man across the river closing his blind.

Now I only watch swallows when they fly in fifteen tangents,
as they break up old sentences,
that could have been perfectly useful
for an essay on the duplicity of identity.

The tangents might make another cloud,
so I can forget and be more like myself
lying under a tabby sky, on a paisley quilt, with you.

Carver's Graveyard Tour

I have been taking Carver's graveyard tour
and we are visiting James Joyce.
Something makes me look directly up
and there is a remarkable bank of straight
cirrus, about three acres of them, at 40,000 feet —
it's like Joyce is up there with Carver
raking the cirrus into neat lines.
They get tired towards the end
and leave some curved and matted clouds
to sit down and have a smoke.

I say, 'Jesus, Raymond.
When are you going to stop smoking?'

James says, 'Same as my daughter Lucia,'
shakes his head
and goes back to raking
til all the threads are lined up.

Architrave

Coming alone into the dark hall, my fingers
cross the architrave, find and move
the small obstinacies
of four toggles on a four-plate switch
and, some steps in, the fluorescent
starters make that happy blinking noise,
four gangs of tubes — each a double —
repeat, one after the other, that greeting
chirrup, which announced all through childhood's
awkward fluorescence, here comes the light,
you're home.

White Poem No 4: Ode to the Potato

First there is peeling, and washing, to find
the white body, which boiling turns
to a soft and floury density, three times
riced, so there is whiteness flopping everywhere,
I beat and begin to understand that dream
where all the spaces between the words
are light, packed with whipped potato
lightness. This is what gives the words
room to think. I beat in soft wads
of butter, warm milk and cream, pyramids of salt
and anticipation, all the cloud air puffs out at me
its warm potato breath, I am balancing perfectly
all the white potato space in between
the scaffolds of real potato.

three puzzle pieces

1.
Thrown into the air, it sings so fine,
a metal puzzle with *bel canto* knots,
I can hear the slight clash jingle
as it slides together at the apex
then its bright ringing descent
before landing on my open hand,
where I consider the two twists,
each clever strand, looped together,
through the gap, by aligning empty space.
Neither piece knows how it locks together
or why it falls apart.

2.
Twenty faded, coloured wooden spheres,
each spindled to two others, a loop with corners,
that slouches pluralistically. As it moves
in three dimensions, I think of it as a wooden model
for an outdated organic compound.
Then my physics mate says
it's a puzzle – he twists and folds for half an hour,
finds a four unit tetrahedron, which falls undone.
He wastes another half going nowhere.
But now I know what it should be, my hands
automatically assemble its perfect 3-D geometry.
Like falling in love with your flat mate – sometimes
the body does things so much better than the head.

3.
A rectangle of wooden blue,
with five tusky yellow banana shapes
in a subtle gradient of sizes,
harder to judge which banana fits
its what banana slot than one might think.
Eight years pass,
I like its look even more than at the start,
and Blu Tak the bananas in, (it's framed already)
and hang it up. Theo explains to friends,
that it was a toy,
but now I have fixed in the bananas
it does nothing and is art.

Night Croquet

Midnight, as the mist descends, the long weekend,
we set out after dinner, leave the fire, take the liquor,
the cold, exquisite, holds my fingers,
the light's oblique as if we see from above.

The earth smells like deep grass and unopened jonquils
the cold exquisite holds my fingers, the pegs are set,
unfulfilled, it's mallet time, we clock and punt
through serried wickets in a damp slipper-ness

of grass. Night croquet is cunning, the ball slides
with an under-hiss, that you can't hear at all,
the distance crowds all around but your feet
are getting further off, well after midnight

the mist slows white, the distance disappears.
My ball glides off into the dark, someone (P) calls, 'Foul,'
and someone loud (T) says, 'You're Cheating.'
It's a jocular, slightly drunk, interlocutory.

I have miles to go. My markers loiter like promises
unkempt. S's back-cut ball jumps P's that blocks
the wicket and rolls through. My fingers are exquisite.
It's night, croquet, the mist envelops.

On a backwater eBay in Seyfert's Galaxy
(Date: BB19.876.45)

'And this, what is this red liquid,
that costs as much as a Moon of Argus?'

The Ikstat is leaning into his console.
He can smell the outrage coming
from the Masli Trader through the screen.

Ikstat Bas says: 'This red liquid? It's a rare code,
dense and Avogadric (Vago Masli humphs) –
You must know the story. This species
from a live planet, Galactic Sector ZZ9 Plural Z Alpha[2].
are trade addicts, so rapacious
they dig up the planet's beams to sell
to each other, burning down their house.
Yes, hard to say why – many are voracious, the rest lazy,
a few are natural coders.
When the Ikstat first noticed them they were sending
streams of code out in all directions...'

'But this is weird, the Plural Z Alpha species,
bipeds (yes, I know the Masli say bipeds are always
of dubious morality), these bipeds think their Burners
are kings, they worship combustion. Their Coders?
Strangely they ignore their Coders and regard them
with the disdain that the Masli hold for Burners.
A crazy species they tried to trade single elements,
lead, and even gold, and then thinking
they were clever, basic machine programs.'

---

[2] Space co-ordinates for Earth from *The Hitchhiker's Guide to the Galaxy*

'Of course the whole Planet fell to moles of hydrogen,
all over carbon. Stripped of atmosphere bits
of Plural Z Alphas and their code were discovered for millennia,
the code form we still use — quite lovely really, but this red fluid?'

Ikstat Bas's feelers sway like hypnotic anemone, one delicately
strokes his left eyebrow, and he shifts forward,
'You might ask what it is not. The colour's
deep from a quadratic of haem and globin,
a molecule that virtually trades in oxygen.
Unload oxygen, it shifts from ruby glow to bluish red.
Then also, this liquid can defend itself, these white cells
teach themselves to destroy invaders.
(Yes, of course, some adaptations will take longer
but you need do nothing, when in place it learns alone.)
Leaks? Self-sealing — there is a myth that the bonds
it forms were so highly rated that lovers
(Lovers? Archaic word — check your OED) cut
their flesh, mingled this, their body fluid,
to seal their flesh together.'

(Vago's wing cases ruffle like brittle paper,
Ikstat Bas coughs, makes the sorry signal
with his hands. Vago sits down.)

'But this stuff, their tribal word for it was blood
a word that meant both ancestors and life.
It is what made them, and crafty, with coding coded
into its neat helicoid. A puzzle, not yet properly unpacked,
that gives all the protein sequencing for the species.
With this you can make filters, pumps, consciousness
– there is a theory that you might even acquire
poetry and music, to create and recombine
seamlessly. Yes, one or two have been re-engineered
but they are not right and all they do is weep.'

Excerpts from the Dictionary of Vago Masli
[Date: BB19.876.55]

Shadowfact
An oscillating element consisting of either graphite powder or boredom, depending on the number of shoes in a biped wardrobe.

Glutenberg
A type of time-space made without a constant fixative which therefore tends to vista-ize between 11 and 27pm, possibly prevented by arriving early with buttered bread held face downwards on outstretched palms.

Starwagonette
Despite the suggestion made in the OED[897th] that this word is derived from artefact transport, it describes a primitive variety of ux-time accelerant traditionally used on long weekends to get through family pixel parties.

Tale
A kind of cabbage that rots before it germinates leaving an odour of old socks in the garden.

Glutenbergers
People who mime the phrase "Are you lucky or what?"; also a kind of half-day police.

Tailer
A person employed to dispel tale seeds from the garden; an hereditary job where national selection has created a race of tailers who can't smell socks or parmesan.

Garnish
To feel temporary loathing for one's limb extremities, expressed in re-colourising fingers, nails or both, and, more rarely, the cutting off of toe nails in bipeds.

Taste
A variety of adhesive dots, the word grew etymologically out of a mix of tar, paste and water which was later refined and sold in small packets.

Taxi
A short blunt knife left outside in the rain.

Tarragon
A quality of prescience in dogs or goldfish that enables them to find where their owners will be going on their next holiday.

Tasmania
A brand of breakfast cereal with extra humidity.

Travel
A kind of ticked coat or fur usually associated with Ibis.

Telepathy
The way in which water will retain the memory of vessels.

Last night, lying there

they cut off my wings, this morning and all day
the blunt and sharp ache of removal

and me, thinking of the days I had flown, in wild wheeling arcs
over the river's lustre, into the green mesmerism of trees

gliding on aileron and thermals, the world bending
below me, the echo of gullies and pins dropping

the spook clouds, settling like opium dust
swept off before I knew enough to be frightened

the night flights through bombed libraries
the days preening my wings' long white quills.

All day the blunt ache, the sharp loss, so I wonder
if it would have been better to be born without them.

www.ingramcontent.com/pod-product-compliance
Lightning Source LLC
LaVergne TN
LVHW041549070426
835507LV00011B/1010